Is It Wednesday Yet?

How to live rent-free, save tax-free,
and escape the rat race by this time next year or sooner!

Wallace R. Curiel
TMG Books

IS IT WEDNESDAY YET?™
Published by TMG Books.
ISBN-13: 978-1463790394
ISBN:-10: 1463790392

Copyright © 2012 by Wallace R. Curiel.

Printed in the United States of America.

10 9 8 7 6 5 4 3 2 1

Is It Wednesday Yet?

…for Daniela…

I love you, Dear!

Preface

The title for this book comes from the one question that is probably asked more than any other in workplaces all across America—*Is it Friday yet?*

This book was written for those who want to work less to live more and in the pages that follow you will learn a simple and workable plan to escape the rat race. You do know what the rat race is, don't you? Well, just in case you don't, let me explain it to you:

The rat race is the five-day, forty-hour workweek.

Why you, personally, want to escape doesn't really matter: The escape-plan detailed in this book works regardless of your motivation. But I warn you—the plan, itself, is so simple that, if you have felt stuck for a long time now, you might feel like kicking yourself for not figuring this out a long time ago yourself.

My plan to work less to live more is this: Work three days a week—simple, right? The most common first-reaction to this plan when someone first hears it is to think, "Yea, right, sorry, but I can't afford the pay cut!"

If that was your first reaction, you will soon see why that is wrong. In fact, working three days-a-week is just one part of an entire lifestyle-design strategy that could well provide you more income after you make the switch to the four-day weekend than you were earning when you were still working five days-a-week.

Welcome to the four-day weekend—

Is it Wednesday yet?

Table of Contents

Introduction

Even if you enjoy your work, the traditional five-day workweek can be a real grind. If you don't like your job, or even if it is only the case that there is something else you would rather be doing, working five days-a-week can be a real drag.

The workday seems to last forever, while weekends seem to fly by. There is so much we need to get done during the weekend that there simply doesn't seem to be enough time to do it all!

I spent years trying to address these issues in my own life. For much of that time, I thought the answer to the stress work caused me was to find more enjoyable work. And, believe me, I tried. In the years I spent in the rat race of the five-day workweek I had four distinct careers and earned five college degrees; all this in search of work that wouldn't seem so much like…well, so much like work!

Then, one day it dawned on me: It wasn't the work that was the problem, it was the fact that I was working much more than I was living.

In my last job before I made my escape, I would get up at six in the morning to be at my desk by eight or so and spend almost an hour each workday on the road. Then I would leave the office sometime after four in the afternoon and, finally, get home at about five.

My work was not physically demanding but it did leave me drained anyway. By the time I made it home, I was not really good for much; a couple of drinks, some television, and, then, to bed so I could rest up to do it again the next day.

What a life! But, again, I really didn't mind the work; after all, I was paid well and the job also had other, more intrinsic rewards that I enjoyed, as well. Work is a good thing, especially if you need the money! But there is such a thing as too much of a good thing and five days-a-week was just that—too much of a good thing.

I fully recognized that good work is an important part of a full life and the workplace fills certain social needs that most of us have. But I didn't need to work five days a week to fulfill those needs. No, the only reason I worked five days a week was that *I thought* I needed five days of income.

But here's the thing in that regard: Throughout that part of my life that I spent working five days-a-week, regardless of how much money I was making at the time, that was how much I spent. And, as my income climbed, so did my expenses and expenditures—funny how it works like that!

About this time, I started to think that the answer to working for a living was financial independence, that is, to have enough money in the bank that the interest it would earn would be enough to completely replace the income I earned by working.

And, yes, financial independence would certainly provide me an escape from the rat race. But when I sat down to figure out how much money I would need to achieve total financial independence the number was staggering.

At the time, my annual income was about $40,000. I determined that in order to replace that amount with interest income, and assuming that I could earn an annual return of 5%, I would need to accumulate a nest egg of $800,000!

If I could manage to sock away, say, 10% of my income a year, I figured I could save that amount in, oh, 200 years or so. Complete financial independence, I quickly came to realize, was a very expensive proposition and might not be the answer I was looking for.

And, besides, it wasn't work I minded, it was it five-day workweek that was wearing me down. What, I wondered, would it do to that $800,000 figure if, instead of giving up on paid employment entirely, I were to work only three days a week?

I did not pluck that three-day workweek out of thin air, by the way. I arrived at it after trying a few different variations on the forty-hour workweek including the four-day workweek and what is known as the 5/4/9 schedule which allows for a four-day workweek every other week.

Neither schedule provided me the balance between work days and free days that I was after. Finally, based on my experience with workweeks of different length, I decided that I wanted more free days than work days and the four-day weekend was the only schedule that would achieve that balance.

Each day of a five-day workweek represents 20% of total income. So, if I worked only three days-a-week, and assuming I made the same hourly wage, I would be earning 40% less. Faced with that shortfall, I realized I had a few options:

1. I could save enough so that the interest earned on those savings would make up that 40% shortfall;

2. I could cut my expenses to the cover the difference, although cutting back by 40% seemed like a stretch;

3. I could find a way to cover the shortfall from some independent source of additional income, or;

4. I could use a combination of those strategies.

Strategy number one was, basically, the alternative to total financial independence and I took to referring to it as *financial freedom.*

And, even before I ran the numbers, I knew financial freedom had to cost significantly less than total financial independence. Instead of needing to *replace* my entire $40,000 annual income, a three-day workweek would cut that number down to $16,000 (40,000 x .4).

During the time I was crunching these numbers it came to me that all you needed to do to arrive at the total amount of the nest egg necessary to provide a given amount of income was to multiply the yearly amount by 20, assuming you could earn a five percent return on your savings or investments. In this case, $16,000 multiplied by 20 equals $320,000.

Still a big number, I know, but it was **less than one-half** of the amount I had, at first, thought I would need.

During this time, it also occurred to me that I would not need to replace 100% of my five-day income. For one thing, I was saving about 10% of income at the time and quickly realized that I wouldn't need to replace that income in order to escape the rat race.

Once I came to this realization, it was something of an *Aha!* moment:

Every dollar of your gross income that you are not spending, when you are working five days-a-week, reduces the amount of income you need to replace once you make the switch to the four-day weekend by that same amount.

So, even though I was earning $40,000 a year at the time, I was saving $4,000 a year. So, at most, the amount of income I would need to replace to be able to "afford" the four-day weekend would be $12,000 *not* $16,000 because I did not need to replace the $4,000 I was saving. This realization brought my "number" (the size of the nest egg necessary to produce the necessary interest income) down to $288,000 ($36,000 x .4 x 20).

Pouring over my check stub, I saw that I was paying almost eight percent of my gross income in employment taxes. Now, as long as I was working, I would be paying that same gross percentage but the absolute amount would be less if I were earning less.

This difference in the amount of taxes I was paying on the income I was earning by working five days-a-week and what I would earn when I was working only three days-a-week would represent additional savings that also would not need to be replaced. I quickly realized that the same principle applied to my state and federal taxes, as well.

As a percentage of income, the tax expense I would avoid simply because I was earning less represented a savings that I estimated would be approximately ten percent. And, again, that ten percent was not income that I would need to replace to maintain the exact same net income after I switched to the three-day workweek.

Adding those tax savings to the ten percent I was already saving, now I only needed to replace 20% ($8,000) of my income with interest income (or some other source) to achieve a four-day weekend level of financial independence. $8,000 times 20 is $160,000.

And, as you can see, the more closely
I examined the figures, the lower the number
dropped!

At this point, I started to take it for granted that it was likely that my number could be reduced even further. I didn't know exactly where to start to look for additional ways to lower my number but I was determined to do so. Could I, for example, save more?

If I could reduce my spending by another ten percent and add that amount to my savings, I would not only reduce the amount of the nest egg I needed, I would also cut the time it would take to save the necessary amount in half!

And if I could, in fact, cut my budget by another ten percent, my number would drop to $80,000. Still, not an insubstantial amount of money, I know, but a number of a different magnitude when compared to the $800,000 I thought I would need at first!

And there were a couple of considerations that made this figure even less daunting: For one thing, I already had a few thousand in the bank; in other words, I wasn't starting to build my nest egg from zero and it is likely that you won't be, either.

For another thing, once I had a firm goal in mind, it was as though the forces of the universe (serendipity?) aligned in my favor (or *something!*) and my nest egg grew by leaps and bounds.

Whereas, before, every windfall, large or small, seemed to simply disappear into spending, now those amounts went straight into my four-day weekend fund.

Eventually, I was able to achieve my goal in less than five years and shortly thereafter was able to make the transition to the four-day weekend. I love it and, if you can relate to any of the issues I had with the five-day workweek, so will you.

But knowing what I know now, and after a number of years trying to figure out how to help others achieve the four-day weekend, I have developed strategies that will make it possible for you escape the rat race by this time next year—or sooner!

These same strategies will also work double-time for you and help you live rent-free and save tax-free while, at the same time, enabling you to achieve total financial independence by the time you reach retirement age, as well.

And, if this all sounds too good to be true, all I can tell you is to keep reading!

Part One

**How to Retire from the Rat Race
By This Time Next Year—or Sooner!**

Chapter One

The Plan in a Nutshell

First of all, let me skip right to the chase here and reveal the basic financial strategy that will make it possible for you to escape the rat race and enjoy a four-day weekend, every week, from now on, for the rest of your working life:

The rat-race-workweek is forty hours of work divided into five, eight-hour days. What that means is that each day represents 20% of your pay for one week's work.

So, if you were to switch to working three eight-hour days, you would, *in theory*, earn three days' pay or 60% of your five-day income; I say, "in theory," because the fact is that part-time jobs often pay a lower hourly wage than full-time jobs.

I will address this issue later and you will learn that it is not as big a deal as it might first appear to be; so, that being the case, I will leave that consideration out of the equation for the time being.

The first element of the plan that deviates from the five-day workweek schedule is that, after making the switch to the four-day weekend (4DW), you will work three, ten-hour days not three eight-hour days. Those three ten-hour workdays are critical to the plan.

Why? Because by working thirty hours a week spread over three days you will be working 75% of your pre-4DW work schedule—not the 60% you would be working (and earning!) if you only worked three, eight-hour days. Here's the math:

5 x 8 = 40; 3 x 10 = 30; 30/40 = .75 (75%).

OK, you're probably thinking, the numbers make sense except for one small problem—I can't afford a 25% cut in pay! This is always the first issue that is raised when I, personally, present this plan to someone or by someone when I present the plan to a group.

First of all, if the plan was totally dependent on the income you will earn by working three days-a-week, the actual difference would almost certainly be *more* than 25%.

Why? Because, as I wrote, part-time jobs almost always pay a lower hourly wage than full-time jobs and the benefits provided part-time employees are not as good as those for full-time employees.

But there is more to my plan than financing your escape from the rat race with only the income from your thirty-hour workweek and, then, there is this:

To maintain the exact same lifestyle you now enjoy, it is only necessary to replace that part of your income that you are, presently, actually spending.

I mentioned this aspect of the plan before but it is one key to the 4DW strategy and I will explore it in more detail, later in the book. And, also later in the book, I will go into depth on all the numbers but those are it in a nutshell.

The last part of the plan I will cover, and, perhaps, the single, most powerful strategy you can use to achieve the four-day weekend is a way to eliminate what is, today, probably the single largest expense in your life.

In fact, by applying this strategy, it is likely that you will be able to turn that expense into a source of additional income and, just maybe, fund your escape entirely!

The expense I am referring to here is the cost of housing and the strategy to eliminate that cost could more than offset the difference in your income before and after making the switch to the four-day weekend.

And, this same strategy will also provide you a way to live rent-free, save tax-free, and to one day achieve total financial independence *and* fund a more financially secure retirement later in life.

Chapter Two

Alternatives to the Four-Day Weekend

Before we get into the nuts and bolts of the plan to achieve four-day weekends for life, let's talk about some of the alternatives to my strategy. There are, basically, two alternatives to the 4DW as a strategy to escape the rat race and those are self-employment and total financial independence.

First of all, self-employment can be preferable to being an employee, but it can also be something of a rat race in itself. When you are self-employed, you will be responsible for all the many tasks that are taken care of for you by the support network you have when you are an employee.

When you are self-employed, getting all those support-tasks accomplished will be work that is, basically, unpaid; that is, it does not provide income and instead it is just more that you will need to do for yourself.

And even if the business is something you love, when you are self-employed you can no longer leave your "work" at the office.

Also, when you are self-employed, a large part of each workday will by necessity be devoted to marketing to attract customers in some form or another.

Marketing is a skill that takes time to learn and even more time to get good at. But marketing—selling, in other words—is not something for which many of us have a natural inclination. And self-promotion—that is, selling ourselves—is something that many of us find even more difficult to do than selling something other than yourself.

I am currently self-employed and I have had a small business on and off since 1980. I have found that there are two secrets to successful self-employment. The first is that, whatever business you choose, it does not require the constant flow of new customers to produce profits; in other words, that the business be one that has repeat-customers.

For example, a restaurant has a lot of customers that come back quite often; repeat business, in other words. A tire shop, on the other hand, might not ever see the same customer twice. It will greatly reduce the amount of on-going marketing required if you can make repeat-customers a feature of your business model.

The second aspect of a good self-employment model is that income is not tied to hours worked. Ideally, a self-employment situation would be producing income even when you are asleep or, better yet, on vacation!

If income is directly tied to labor, like being a plumber or accountant or any other form of self-employment like those, then if you don't work you don't earn.

I discovered a small-business model that fit the bill in both regards and you will learn what it is as we proceed.

The second alternative to the 4DW to escape the rat race is total financial independence (TFI). First, let me define financial independence: You are financially independent when you have a source of income other than paid employment sufficient to meet your income requirements.

And, if you think about it, you will realize that retirement requires financial independence, but you do not need to be of "retirement age" to be financially independent. TFI would, certainly, be great but total financial independence will most often be a very expensive proposition, indeed!

As I mentioned before, I once considered trying to achieve total financial independence in order to escape the rat race. My thinking at that time was influenced, mostly, by the book, *Your Money or Your Life*, written by Joe Dominguez and Vicki Robin.

In that book, the authors detail a strategy to achieve total financial independence. I recommend you read that book, not for that strategy, in particular, but for some of the other steps they detail as part of the lifestyle they advocate.

I still believe that planning to achieve total financial independence should be part of a long-term financial plan and I did, in fact, eventually achieve total financial independence although I keep working anyway. But I know now that it is not necessary to do so in order to achieve the "work less to live more" goal of the 4DW.

And, besides the size of the nest egg required to achieve total financial independence and the time it would take most of us to save the required amount, there were still more problems with TFI as a means of escape from the rat race—namely, inflation and the likelihood that your returns would not always meet the amount necessary to preserve your capital.

When the income from your nest egg was sufficient or greater than your expenditures, this issue would not present a problem. But in those years when your returns were less than your cost of living, then it would present a *very* big problem.

And, if you had a few consecutive years like that, you would wind up spending your capital to meet your income needs. Doing that, spending your capital, would likely result in insufficient returns from that point forward and you could, ultimately, run out of money!

The other problem is inflation. If your expenses are (x) today, and inflation averages only three percent a year for five consecutive years, your expenses will be [(x) times 1.16] in five years' time. And, your expenses will be going up that three percent and then some every year between now and then, due to the effect of compounding!

What inflation means in the real world is that your nest egg will probably not be enough even if you manage to achieve the assumed five percent return.

This, I realized, presented something of a sticky wicket but it was not the single most glaring issue with total financial independence as the means to escaping the rat race. Again, the real problem was that number, itself— the $800,000 necessary to fund total financial independence!

At the time, I pushed forward anyway on my plan to achieve TFI because what I had discovered was that working towards any goal was a lot like driving at night; that is, you can only see as far as your head lights reach but the way forward is illuminated as you proceed.

I fully expected my path to escaping the rat race to be revealed in much the same way. And so it was! You now know that switching from the forty-hour, five-day workweek to the four-day weekend will, at first glance, seem to result in a 25% loss of income. I have already told you, however, that that is not the case. Let me now explain that claim to you.

Chapter Three

What the Switch to Four-Day Weekends Will Really Cost

Those of us who have a job to earn a living think we know what we are paid, when in fact, we seldom know how much we *really* earn. The best way to make my point here is to consider what you earn by the hour.

So, for example, if you make $32,000 a year, you earn about $16 an hour. The basic math here is as follows: 40 hours per week times 52 weeks = 2,080 paid hours per year. $16 an hour times 2080 = $33,280. Of course, this higher amount assumes that you take no unpaid vacation or sick leave so, for the sake of this example, we will round down to $32,000 and an actual hourly rate, based on 2,080 of paid hours, of $15.38

Of course this is the amount you will *gross*, that is, the amount you earn before taxes are deducted. The amount you have left after taxes are deducted is what is known as your "net" pay.

All earned income is subject to, what is known as, employment taxes. Employment taxes are paid to fund your future Social Security and Medicare benefits. In 2010 those two employment taxes totaled 7.65% of gross pay and in this example those deductions would total $2,448.

Now, to look at it from another perspective, those "employment" taxes reduce your actual income to a little more than $14 an hour; here's the math:

$32,000 minus $2,448 = $29,552 divided by 2080 = $14.20 an hour.

Remember, when we started this exercise, your gross hourly wage was $15.38; that has already been reduced by over one dollar an hour!

To continue to compute your "real" hourly wage, all you do is, first, identify all the costs you pay for the "privilege" of working and, then, subtract those costs from the amount of your gross pay.

Now, continuing with the effect of taxes and how they reduce your net income, let's assume that your total tax liability, including Federal, state, and employment taxes, is 20%.

(20% is, by the way, fairly representative of the national average based on 2009 Bureau of Labor Statistics data.)

When we subtract that 20% from your gross pay, the net after taxes is now down to $25,600 or about $12.30 an hour.

The next consideration I like to apply to arrive at "real" wage is actual number of hours worked. So, for example, if we assume that, between commuting and getting ready, your work day is actually ten hours long, then instead of dividing your net after taxes by 2080 (40 x 52), you need to divide it by 2,600 hours (50 x 52).

The result of that computation would be ($25,600/2600) = $9.84.

There are other subtractions you will need to make in order to arrive at your own "real" wage. After taxes and actual hours worked, the next biggest considerations for most people are transportation and child care.

Child care can, sometimes, reduce real wages to next to nothing! And, if you pay child care in order to work, figuring out what is left after child care could really open your eyes.

The cost of child care will not apply to everyone but one cost that will apply almost universally is that of transportation.

One organization, commutesolutions.org, has computed the cost of driving one mile to be $1.19. The Automobile Association of America, on the other hand, puts this number at about seventy-eight cents per mile.

For the sake of this example, we will assume a number in the middle of those two: Ninety-eight and one-half cents per mile.

Now, to figure out your annual work-related expenses attributable to transportation costs, you simply multiply the number of miles of work-related driving you do every week times the 52 weeks in a year and, then, multiply that number by the assumed cost per mile of .985.

So, let's assume your weekly total of work-related driving is fifty miles; the math would look like this:

50 x 52 = 2,600 mile of work-related driving per year time (.985 cost per mile) = $2,561. Now we subtract that from the previous balance of $25,600 and we are left with $23,039 or slightly more than $8.86 an hour.

Looking at this number another way, almost half of the gross pay in this example is lost to the job-related costs of income and employment taxes, actual hours worked, and transportation!

Of course, even when you switch to the four-day weekend, these same costs will still apply except for one very key consideration: They will be *proportionally less*. And this is a very important consideration, indeed, on your path to the four-day weekend as I will explain in a later chapter.

The reaction to this information is often something along the lines of, "What does it matter how much or, rather, how *little* I make an hour, I need all I earn whether it's $16 or $8—I can't afford a pay cut!" Look, I feel your pain. But what is gained from computing your real wage in this way is a new perspective when you take and apply that number to your everyday purchases and recurring costs of living.

For example, let's say the numbers above apply to someone paying $80 a month for cable TV. What that means is that, when your real wage is $8.86 an hour, you will need to work in excess of one full day just to pay your cable bill every month! And it is only when you do know your real wage that you can begin to judge the relative value of the individual components of your cost of living and the real cost of any purchase you are considering.

A new $1,200 television, for example, will require that you work almost 150 hours—almost a full month! Look—life is made up of time. Most of us will have something like 72 years of time and all of our balances are already well below that number by now. Do you really want to spend an entire month of your life working in order to buy a new TV?

I can't answer that for you but, once you know your real wage, you will have the information you need to answer that question for yourself.

But the most important consideration, when you are aware of your real wage, is that it makes you think about how you are, in fact, trading time for consumption. And this thought, in turn, I hope will lead you to this conclusion: Perhaps the single, most simple way by which you can buy back your time in order to be able to "afford" the four-day weekend is by reducing consumption!

> *Frugality is like a sort of financial alchemy that turns expenses into freedom!*

If you are able to reduce your cost of living to what you would earn working thirty hours a week instead of forty hours a week—and I believe that almost all of us can do that without it having much, if any, of an impact on our quality of life—you could make the switch to the four-day weekend about as soon as it takes to pack up your desk at work!

Chapter Four

More Four-Day Weekend Math

So, we have already established that, by switching to three ten-hour work days, you will be able to replace, dollar for dollar, 75% of what you were earning when you worked a five eight-hour-days schedule.

But here is where the math gets a little tricky because common sense would tell you that, based on the basic math of the equation, the four-day weekend would leave you 25% short, right? Wrong!

Remember, your taxes will be lower when you earn less and almost all of your work-related expenses will be less when you work two fewer days every week, as well. Exactly how much those costs will total depends on a few variables unique to each individual situation but, using the numbers from the previous example, we can get an idea of what the numbers will look like.

And, again, the key here is this: You do not need to replace income that you were not previously spending in support of your life style. The easiest way to show you what I mean by this is by using the example of savings.

If you are saving ten percent of your gross income, for example, that is money that is not going to support your lifestyle.

What that means is that when you made the switch to the four-day weekend and three-day workweek, the most income you would need to replace in order to net enough to afford the exact same level of consumption would be 90% of your previous income.

And, so, if we assume that by working three, ten-hour days you will replace 75% of your previous income, you could subtract the 10% you are saving from that 25% because *you are not spending it now*! And, so, you would only need to replace 15% of your previous income, at most.

The bottom-line is this: After you switch to the four-day weekend and the thirty-hour workweek, you will only need to replace 100% of the income you were actually spending when you worked forty hours a week.

Now back to our example of someone earning $32,000 a year:

If that person was saving 10% of that amount, $3,200, they would only need to replace $28,800 or 90% of what they were earning before making the switch to the four-day weekend.

Assuming a post-four-day weekend income of $24,000, having a savings rate of 10% would mean your income after making the switch would be equal to almost 85% of your full-time paycheck.

Suddenly, the difference has gone from 25% to 15%!

Again, you don't need to replace any income that is not going to support your lifestyle; that is, you do not need to replace any income that is not going to pay the bills and fund your other spending.

And what is an example of money you are earning but that is not being spent to support your cost of living? Savings!

Of course, I am assuming here that you will want or need to replace 100% of what you are now spending based on your desire to maintain the exact same level of consumption after you make the switch to the four-day weekend as you had when you were still working five days-a-week.

But I have found that, in most cases, it's easier to simply reduce spending by finding lower cost alternatives or, simply, to cut items from your budget than it is to replace income dollar-for-dollar! After all, in most cases, the actual dollar amount will not be much.

And, perhaps, the most simple and easy way to make the switch to the four-day weekend is to reduce your expenses until they are equal to what you will be earning when you are working thirty hours a week instead of forty. Once you do that, you can fearlessly ditch the rat race!

And, besides, in most cases the difference in net pay will amount to 10% *or less* of whatever you are earning now. If you are already saving that much or more, guess what?

You can switch to the four-day weekend about as soon as you can arrange the switch to working three, ten-hour days!

Chapter Five

Escape for Ten Cents on the Dollar!

So, the next question is: How did I arrive at 10% as the shortfall between a thirty hour workweek and forty hour workweek? Well, let's go back to the numbers in our example scenario:

We are assuming a gross income of $32,000 and a tax rate of twenty percent or $6,400 a year.

If we now assume that we are earning 75% after switching to the four-day weekend, our new gross is $24,000. If we apply the same tax rate to that amount, we will pay a total of $4,800 a year.

But the thing is, and this is a very, very big deal here: You don't need replace that extra $1,600 you used to pay in taxes.

In other words, you can, *in effect*, add that amount back to your post-4DW income because you will "net" the same buying power. $1,600 is equal to five percent of $32,000 and that five percent can be added to the 75% you will be earning when you make the switch to working three ten-hour days.

What that means is that you are earning the equivalent of 80% of your previous buying-power simply because, when you earn less, you will pay less in taxes. And, in fact, the difference could be greater than 5% because you might be in a lower tax bracket! Actually, as far as I am concerned we could stop right here. I mean, in my opinion, 20% of your income is not much to pay for double the free time of four-day weekends for life!

But, in fact, the money you will save by working and, so, *commuting* two days less every week, should easily add up to another five percent. This will serve to make your effective net closer to 85% and the shortfall a measly 15%!

Let's say you are willing to give up 5% of your previous gross income (by way of reducing and/or eliminating some expenses) as a fair price for double the free time. In that case, all I need to do is to show you how to reduce your present cost of living by ten percent to enable your switch to the four-day weekend, right?

Right, so let's get to it!

Chapter Six

Preparing to Launch!

First, before I explain how to make up the 10% difference between your present income and your income when you are enjoying a four-day weekend every week, let me give you a few pointers on preparing for the four-day weekend.

First of all, you should have some cash or the equivalent of cash readily available in case of an emergency that will make such a "rain-day" fund necessary.

The question, then, is this: How much do you need to have in reserve? Well, the easy answer to that is the more the better but I recommend that you have an amount equal to at least three months of living expenses.

How did I decide on this amount?

Well, this money is there primarily in case you lose your job and I figure, between unemployment benefits and your rainy-day fund, you should have enough to last you at least six months of 100% income replacement. And, I also figure, six months should be enough time to find a new part-time—thirty hours-a-week—job.

And, by the way, it is usually much easier to find part-time employment than it is to find a full-time job.

My second tip is that you should manage your finances using a monthly budget and that you include a line item in your budget for a certain amount of monthly savings that will keep your rainy-day fund growing.

If you don't presently use a budget to manage your money, I strongly urge you to start doing so before switching to the four-day weekend. Why?

Well, I believe that it is better to be a prudent steward of your resources and part of being that prudent steward is that you are "in-touch" with the flow of money into and out of your life.

The ancient philosopher, Seneca, wrote that, "no wind favors a ship without a destination." I mean, that is just common sense, right? And the opposite of that dynamic, call it luck or serendipity, is a force you want to have working for you not against you.

A budget is simply a plan for how you will deploy your financial resources to achieve your financial *goals*; and what is a goal, after all, but a *destination*, of sorts?

I have been using a monthly budget to run my finances for over twenty years now; it is practically a habit and I know now for a fact that however I was managing my money before I started using a budget was the reason I had a major financial meltdown when I was in my early thirties. So, you need a rainy-day fund and a plan for every dollar that enters your life—that plan is called a monthly budget.

The third thing you will need when you make the switch to four-day weekends is a plan for how you will spend all your new free time.

No problem, right? Well, what I discovered, after I achieved total financial independence and quit all paid employment entirely, was that I was not as prepared as I could have been to make the most of all the new time I had on my hands.

At first, my to-do list of projects kept me pretty busy. But, then, after about a year, I had totally cleared my to-do list and, suddenly, I had all this time! Eventually, I got a little bored and I even thought of going back to work full-time.

I did, however, almost immediately come to my senses. I did go back to work but I returned to working only three days-a-week. This largely took care of the boredom I had felt there for a while. But, still, four days is a long time, as you will discover when you make the switch yourself.

At first, you might want to just relax and sort of bask in your new found freedom. And that's fine. In fact, you could use those first couple of months of four-day weekends to develop a plan for your new schedule.

But you should, at the very least, have a good idea in mind for what your life will look like once you make the switch *before* you actually do make the switch.

Finally, I want to touch on the subject of health insurance. You need to have a plan in place to address this issue before you leave the world of full-time employment, particularly if the job you plan on leaving is what now provides you your health insurance.

So, how do you plan for the cost of health insurance? The answer is simply that you budget for it like any other line item in your post-rat race budget. As simple as that sounds, however, in the real world the solution is not so neat or simple simply because there are so many issues that can complicate the matter on a personal level.

For example, if you have a pre-existing condition that might preclude you from getting an individual policy, you must proceed very carefully in making the decision to leave the job that now provides you coverage.

This also applies if anyone else in your family (your spouse or kids, as applicable) has a pre-existing condition. In such a case, the prudent move might well be to keep working.

Paul Terhost, author of the book, *Cashing in On the American Dream*, writes that he pays for routine medical care out of pocket and has a policy for catastrophic coverage in Argentina where, he writes, the medical care is similar in quality to that in the US but the policy, itself, is less costly than it would be here.

At present, I live close to Mexico and I do get some of my health care services there; I realize that this is probably not an option for many of you who are reading this but it is one way I save money in this regard. For example, I went to a US dentist and got an estimate of $1,200 to get a wisdom tooth extracted. I ended up going to Mexico and had it removed for just $50!

One should shop for health care just like any other service or product in order to find the best "deal." And one can bargain for medical services, as well.

Even after health insurance reforms passed in 2010, there is no single or simple solution to this issue. But those seeking to escape the rat race are not a typical lot. We already tend to think outside the box in many ways and this is one more area in which that kind of thinking will need to be applied.

If you are single, your approach can be considerably less conservative, I think, than if someone is dependent on you for their well-being in this regard. But, even if you are without dependents, it doesn't mean you aren't taking a big financial risk if you choose to go without health insurance.

For most of us the answer will be some sort of policy to cover the real possibility of a catastrophic event and paying for the routine expenses out-of-pocket by means of a form of self-coverage, say five or ten thousand dollars in reserve.

The next step will be to think yourself through a worst case scenario: What if? Then carefully consider how you will fare in that situation assuming the contingencies you plan to have in-place.

Another issue with health care costs is that they are rising so fast that they will drive the total annual inflation figure you use in your budgeting calculations through the roof.

Health insurance can be, and has been, a deal breaker for many who would otherwise consider ditching their full-time job.

So, there they are, the four *items* every four-day weekender needs to pack for his or her new life of less work and more life: A rainy-day fund, a monthly budget, a plan for how you will address your health insurance needs, and, last but not least, a plan for how you will make the most of all your new free time!

Chapter Seven

Making Up the Difference

The best way to make up the difference between what you earn now and what you will earn when you make the switch to four-day weekends is to reduce your cost of living by ten percent *right now*—while you are still working five days-a-week!

By doing so, there will not be any need to replace that income. It really is as simple as that and, if you are already saving that much or more, then it is likely that you are already financially able to make the switch to the four-day weekend right now!

If you are not saving that much now, you need to begin to consider every line item in your budget as a place to reduce or, even, eliminate spending. The extent to which you cut and which specific line items you decide to cut will depend on your schedule for making the switch to the 4DW.

The sooner you want to make the switch, the more spending is on the table. I would say that almost all of us waste at least five percent of our income. Money you are now spending to buy back time is one example of wasteful spending; take fast food meals, for example.

Mostly we resort to fast food and even most restaurant meals because our jobs leave us either too little time or energy to make meals at home. Spending we do to buy back time like this is a good place to begin looking for budget reductions because they represent "low-hanging fruit" ready to be plucked from your budget.

One way to begin the process of closely reviewing your spending is to keep, what I call, a spending diary. That is also the title of my book on this subject, *The Spending Diary*.

In that book, I go into greater detail on how to keep a spending diary, how to use it to spot wasteful spending, and also how to identify that spending that can most easily be reduced or eliminated. There are also a number of blank Spending Diary pages so you can begin tracking your spending right away.

A spending diary will also help you to see your own spending patterns and, like a monthly budget, it is a great tool to put you in-touch with the money in your life.

But whatever tool you use, it should not present much of a challenge to find the necessary ten percent, especially if you are highly motivated to make the switch as soon as possible!

And, again, one-half of that ten percent will likely be money you spend to buy back time in the form of convenience. How hard can it be, then, to find the remaining five-percent?

Chapter Eight

Making up the Difference, Continued

One option to cutting your budget by the necessary amount is to find a way to earn an additional ten percent (or whatever the amount of the difference is in your particular situation) after you make the switch to four-day weekends.

Ideally, this extra income will be in place before you make the switch.

One way to do that is to look for a way to, in effect, reduce an expense by using an asset to produce "passive" income, that is, money that is not received as compensation for hours worked. For example, let's say you have a spare bedroom in your house.

For the sake of this example, it makes no difference if you own the house outright, are making mortgage payments, or you are renting the house.

If, for example, your cost of housing is $1,000 a month and that represents 25% of your monthly income (which is, by the way, the national average based on 2009 BLS data), that amount is fixed to the extent that you can't reduce the monthly cost.

But if you were to rent the spare bedroom for, say, $300 a month, you have accomplished the same end— which is to make up for the difference between your income working five days-a-week and your income after you make the switch to the four-day weekend.

And, by the way, if you were to do the math, you would discover that $300 would be equal to 7.5% of the gross amount of your five-day income (the $32,000 we assumed for the sake of example) and would, almost by itself, make up the difference once you made the switch.

I think you will find that finding the "magic" ten percent will be more like a game than any real stretch. In fact, once you put your mind to it, I would not be surprised if you were able to actually save money even after making the switch by reducing your spending even more than ten percent!

And, as you will learn, the best place to make up the difference is by reducing or, even, totally eliminating your expenses for income taxes and housing!

Chapter Nine

It Is Not a Question of Money

So, as you have just seen, the determining factor on whether or not it is possible for you to make the switch to the four-day weekend is seldom money. The money part will probably not, in fact, represent much of a challenge, actually.

Let me here quickly recap the numbers:

The last time we went through this exercise, we assumed that you would be earning the same hourly wage before and after making the switch to the four-day weekend. This time, however, I want to raise the bar a little to make it reflect a sort of worst-case scenario.

If you will remember, I wrote that part-time jobs do not usually pay as much as full-time jobs. And what that means in the real world is that when you cut back to working thirty hours a week, it is possible, even likely, that your hourly wage will be lower.

How much lower? Well, the only way to know for certain is to make the switch. But for the sake of example, and using the same full-time income as in previous examples, let's assume your part-time hourly wage will equal 80% of your full-time hourly wage.

We have already established that an annual salary of $32,000 is equal to an hourly wage of $16. So, when you make the switch to a part-time job your hourly wage will be $12.80 or $384 a week and $19,968 a year. This amount is equal to 62.4% of what you were earning working full-time ($32,000).

First, let's add back the effect of taxes:

Assuming the same 20% tax rate that we have been assuming in all previous examples, you paid $6,400 in taxes on $32,000 of income but would only pay $3,994 (rounding up slightly) after making the switch.

Working full-time, then, you paid $2,406 more in taxes and, adding that back to your part-time income, your actual spending power is equal to $22,374 or 70% after making the switch to the four-day weekend.

Now, let's assume two things:

One, that we can reduce our spending by 10% and, two that that by working two fewer days every week we will reduce the costs related to working by 5%. These two reductions represent $3,200 and $1,600, respectively, for a total of $4,800.

Now, when we "add-back" that amount to our income after making the switch our spending power is not equivalent to $27,174 or 85% of our full-time income!

So, how do we make up the 15% difference? Well, if you will remember, I have previously suggested that you find some way to generate enough passive income to make up the difference. If you were able to do so, you could then make a financially painless transition to the four-day weekend.

And, if you are presently saving some percentage of your income, that is money that will not need to be replaced once you make the switch. And if, for example, you are presently saving 10% of your gross income, the cost of making the switch to the four-day weekend would only be a 5% reduction on spending power. What's the big deal!

And, finally, one last method to span the shortfall would be to make up the difference with income on your nest egg. Using the details of our example, 15% would equal $4,800 and require a nest egg of $96,000 earning 5% interest.

Of course, there actually is one more way to make up the difference and that is some combination of the previous three methods mentioned.

Regardless, I hope that by now you see that it is entirely possible to double your free time and it doesn't mean that you will need to radically alter your standard of living downward. In fact, you should be able to make the transition fairly painless!

But there is one more alternative that I have not yet mentioned: How much more feasible would the four-day weekend be, and how much more attractive would it be to you, personally, if I could show you a way that would make the switch cost-free? What if I could show you a way to finance the four-day weekend without having to cut your budget at all?

Again, in most instances, the easiest, most straight-forward way to make the switch would be to increase the percentage of your income that you are saving by simply reducing your expenses while you are still working at your full-time job—but there is also another way!

And, although the strategy you are about to learn is certainly more involved than simply cutting your spending a little, the additional effort it requires will be well-rewarded.

Part Two

**How to Live Rent-Free
and Save Tax-Free**

Chapter Ten

A Worst Case Scenario

OK, you have seen in one example where the actual difference in income between working five days-a-week and working a part-time, three days-a-week will be about 10%.

Then, in what I referred to as the worst-case scenario, where you took a 20% cut in your the hourly wage, the difference in income was equal to 15% of what was your full-time income.

But, 10% or 15%, I would be willing to wager that you never dreamed that doubling your free time would cost you so little, right? And, still, it is possible that you think you can't afford to make the switch. But what if you could eliminate the cost of housing?

If you could do that, and I will show you that it is, in fact, entirely possible to do that, those savings, alone, would be enough to finance your switch to the four-day weekend.

Of course, I am assuming here that the percentage of your income that you spend on housing now is even close to the national average. How much is the national average?

Well, according to the Bureau of Labor Statistics, the average *household* income in the USA in 2009 was $63,091 before taxes and $49,638 after taxes. (This data was published in 2009 and was the latest information available as of this edition of this book.)

The Bureau of Labor Statistics (BLS) is an agency of the Federal government and there is some additional information you need to know about the data they publish:

The BLS refers to the average American household as a "consumer-unit" and the average consumer-unit is, according to the BLS, one in which there are 2.5 "consumers" and 1.2 "earners."

The $32,000 figure I have been using in the examples is roughly one-half the BLS figure because I assume only a single-income, single-consumer household; of course, your mileage may vary.

Again, the average household income was $63,091 before taxes and $49,638 after taxes. In other words, the average tax bill is almost 22% of gross income; slightly more, in fact, than the 20% we have been using in our examples.

But taxes do not represent the largest single expense in the average budget; that distinction goes to housing which consumes over 34% of the average budget.

But even if your own cost of housing is only one-half of that amount, say 17% of your gross income, if you could cut that cost by half, then the switch to four-day weekends would be absolutely cost-free! In fact, you would even have more net income after making the switch!

And you can, absolutely, cut your cost of housing by 50% or more simply by choosing to make a single change. And that change, simply put, is to make your primary residence one unit in a multi-unit residential property instead of the whole of a single-family residence.

Chapter Eleven

Thinking and Living Outside the Box

Look, living the four-day weekend is something of an alternative lifestyle that requires that you think "outside the box," so to speak. The decision to ditch full-time employment for the luxury of time afforded by the four-day weekend might not represent thinking that is way out there but it is, certainly, at least a little different.

For one thing, most people simply accept the five-day workweek as some sort of gospel or a natural law that is etched in stone—it is not! In fact, the five-day workweek is a fairly recent human construct created by Henry Ford, founder of the Ford Motor Company, not all that long ago.

And, likewise, when most people are in the market to buy a home, the tendency is to lock-in on the idea of a single family residence as the only logical option because that is just how most people think.

Single-family residences are, in fact, the single most expensive form of housing that there is; you can, however, greatly reduce or, even, eliminate the cost of housing by, once again, thinking—*just a little*—outside the box.

And that sort of flexibility of thought will lead you, I believe, to the wisdom of multi-unit residential property as your primary residence.

First, let me define what a "multi-unit residential property" is for you. An MRP (**m**ulti-unit **r**esidential **p**roperty) is otherwise known as an apartment building. The term applies to residential housing with any number of units from two on up.

An MRP with two individual rental units is commonly referred to as a duplex; an MRP with three individual rental units as a triplex; and an MRP with four individual rental units as a fourplex. A multi-unit residential property with more than four individual units will usually be referred to simply as an apartment building.

The rental income from a single rental unit could be sufficient to lower your housing costs to zero. That was the case for me when I purchased a duplex, as I will detail later in this section of the book.

Depending on the particulars of any situation, however, such as local rents and purchase price, a duplex might or might not be sufficient to do so in every case.

In those instances where a duplex is not sufficient to lower your housing cost to zero, a triplex or fourplex will usually do the job. In most cases, however, you will not need to go beyond a fourplex unless you want to turn a profit from your rental business.

And let me also tell you at this point that owning rental property business is just that: A business!

I am always amazed the lengths that people will go to when they are scouting for a small business opportunity. The book, *Acres of Diamonds*, is a classic in the field of self-help/self-improvement. In that book, the author, Russell H. Conwell, tells the story of a man who goes off in search of riches. Years later, he returns to his home, having failed in his mission and later, still, he dies.

Sometime after those events, the new owner of the man's property sees a shiny object on the ground that turns out to be a diamond! As it turns out, the property is a diamond mine filled with the precious jewels.

The moral of the story, obviously, is that the best place to look for your fortune is in your own backyard.

That is certainly true when it comes to real estate and the business opportunity owning a multi-unit residential property affords you!

Right now, right where you live, there are real estate opportunities to be had. And if you find the idea of owning a small-business with unlimited potential for growth, owning rental property is one of the best small business opportunities available.

Chapter Twelve

A Random Walk Down Main Street

In order to show you just how smart it is to own a multi-unit residential property as your primary residence instead of a single-family property, you must first understand the concept of multiple streams of rental real estate income.

The topic of multiple streams of income is all the rage on the internet these days, but it is nothing new. In fact, landlords have been enjoying multiple streams of income ever since the first apartment building was built.

A residential real estate investment has the potential to create six distinct and individual income streams:

1. Rental income;

2. Tax savings from depreciation (don't worry if you don't understand all these terms, we'll get to that);

3. Tax savings for mortgage interest deduction;

4. Equity build-up through paying down the amount of the mortgage;

5. Increased equity through appreciation of the value of the property and;

6. Imputed income.

There is no other investment that offers the same sort of financial leverage that can be obtained from a single residential real estate investment; specifically, a multi-unit residential property owned as your primary residence and in which you occupy one of the units and rent the other(s).

You have probably heard it said that two can live as cheaply as one. Well, that is that same principle that applies when your primary residence is part of an MRP.

And a complex as small a duplex (two units; you live in one of the units and rent the other), a triplex (three units; you live in one of the units and rent the other two), or a fourplex (four units; you live in one of the units and rent the other three) can be all that is required. In other words, you don't need to own some huge apartment complex to live rent-free!

Chapter Thirteen

My Real Estate Story

Somehow, I ended up with a bunch of money. To figure out exactly how this came to be, I thought about it for a while and, then, did some forensic accounting on my bank records.

In doing so, I discovered a period when my savings grew dramatically. It was during the years after I bought a duplex (a house comprised of two separate living units—basically, two apartments although one of the "apartments" was 1,800 square feet and the other 1,000 square feet) in Calexico, CA.

I bought the property in 1999. That was towards the end of a period when real estate values had been declining for a couple of years.

I had paid $109,000 for it and that was a great deal even by the standards of the time. The total of my monthly payment was just about $900. This figure includes principal and interest on the mortgage and property taxes and insurance (PITI), as well. That figure does not, however, include monthly maintenance.

I lived in one of the two apartments and rented the other for $800 a month. Because expenses related to the portion of the house I was renting were considered business expenses by the IRS, I was able to deduct some expenses including a part of the mortgage payment and property taxes I was paying.

In effect, those deductions added to my income on the property through tax savings. Rent and tax savings made it so that I was effectively living there for free; that being the case, I was able to save what I would have otherwise been paying in housing expenses—almost $12,000 a year!

Chapter Fourteen

My Story Gets Even Better!

We lived in that house for almost four years and, in that time, because I was living rent-free, I managed to save over $50,000. Then, when I moved to another state, I sold it for $189,000 and realized a net profit of approximately $80,000.

In a little less than four years my net worth grew by almost $150,000! And 100% of that amount was the direct result of owning and then selling that property.

I sometimes wish, however, that I had kept the house. Why do I say that? Well, consider this: That $150,000 is still in the bank and, at the time I am writing this, it is earning about two percent a year in interest. In other words, about $300 a month before taxes.

When I sold the place, I was getting $850 a month in rent, almost three times as much as the money is earning sitting in the bank! Money in the bank is great but it is a depreciating asset, especially if you are withdrawing any amount to cover living expenses.

The money I "withdrew" as rent was not depreciating the asset-value of the property, itself. In fact, the value of the property appreciated for the entire time I owned it as evidenced by the fact I sold it for a gain of over 40%!

I also realize that if I had kept the property when I moved, I could have rented out the side in which I had been living for $1,200 a month or so (it was larger than the other apartment). And here is one final consideration: I "bought" the property with only 10% down. My down payment and escrow and other closing fees came to a total of just about $12,000. In other words, had I kept the property, I could have been making $2,050 a month on an "investment" of $12,000. A return of over 200% a year!

And rent appreciates. That is, every so often, you can raise the rent you charge. What that means is that not only would my income be rising, so would my net worth as the property, itself, increased in market value.

Selling that property was almost the exact equivalent of killing a goose that laid golden eggs!

Chapter Fifteen

The Moral of My Story

There are a couple of ways for you to achieve rent-free living but, first, let me explain the term, itself: When I use the term, "rent-free," what I mean is that your actual cost of housing is zero or, even, that your housing *arrangement* earn some income for you!

Even if you have a mortgage, if the total of the rents you receive is enough to pay your monthly mortgage payment, you are living rent-free!

The most efficient way to achieve rent-free living is to "own" a property that has two or more individual living units.

Again, let me define the term in quotes in the previous line: When I use the word "own" what I mean is that you acquire beneficial use of the property by means of a mortgage; you don't "own" the property outright but, rather, in partnership with the mortgage lender.

However, for all intents and purposes, a mortgage-lender will allow you to do anything you want with the property. The secret to living rent-free in such a situation is to live in one of the units and to rent out the other(s).

The key to rent-free living will be the income on the unit(s) you rent out (the "rental unit" or rental units, if there are more than the one unit you live in and one unit you rent to someone else). And, the more income you receive from the rental unit or units, the more it will offset your own housing costs—and it might even make you a profit!

But wait, you say, "I don't have the money to buy a house!" Well, there is a way around that: Start a rooming house in a rented house. Let me explain:

If you were to rent, say, a four bedroom house and rent out three of the bedrooms, you might be able to accomplish the same goal: Reduce your cost of housing, maybe even to zero.

Turning a house intended for one family into a rooming house is really easy to do in a neighborhood where there is a college or university nearby but it can be done (and has been done and made to work) in almost any community.

Chapter Sixteen

Let Your Roomies Pay Your Rent!

The mechanics of setting up a rooming house are not *real* simple but neither are they particularly difficult. And it could well be worth your time and effort as a means to the end of the four-day weekend.

Perhaps the hardest part will be to find a landlord willing to let you rent his or her property for the purpose of using it as a rooming house—difficult, maybe, but not impossible!

In the real estate business there is a term applied to people who are desperate to sell their house: They are known as "motivated sellers." Well, there is also such a thing as a motivated landlord.

A motivated landlord is someone who bought another house before they sold their previous house and, so, is making two mortgage payments. They actually want to sell their house but they have been unable to do so and, so, they are forced into becoming landlords to try and make ends meet until the market turns around.

Since the on-going housing implosion began, there are more and more of these motivated landlords out there. And, because these motivated landlords did not go into the rental business on purpose, they are also, what I call, *accidental* landlords.

The crash in housing market has created thousands of accidental landlords and, so, has also created something of a glut in the rental market. In this environment, your chances are good of finding a motivated landlord willing to rent you their property to run as a rooming house. The key is to present yourself to the property owner as a serious person with a sound plan.

I helped an acquaintance find and set-up a rooming house and we had no problem at all finding a motivated landlord. All I did was to place an ad on Craigslist in the "housing wanted" section.

The ad read: Mature individual seeks three or four bedroom house to share with three roommates. We actually received several calls and the only accommodation was a slightly larger deposit. Then, we simply went right back to Craigslist and ran an ad to find the actual roommates.

For more detailed information on running a rooming house, I recommend the book, *Managing Your Rental House for Increased Income*, written by Doreen Bierbrier.

But running a rooming house in a rented property should only be used as a short-term solution. You really want to be an owner because owning the property, whether outright or with a mortgage, is the best way to unleash the power of multiple streams of real estate income!

Chapter Seventeen

A Closer Look at Each Stream

Again, rental real estate has the potential to produce six individual streams of income either as cash or by growing your net worth. They are as follows:

1. Rental income;
2. Tax savings from depreciation (don't worry if you don't understand all these terms, we'll get to that);
3. Tax savings from interest deduction of mortgage interest;
4. Equity build-up through paying down the principal balance of the mortgage;
5. Increased equity through appreciation of the value of the property and;
6. Imputed income.

The thing is, this is only the case when you own the property. These same benefits will not all apply when you run a rooming house in a rented property although a rooming house can provide you with all the benefits of owning a small business including cash income and tax savings.

Most real estate manuals list only four streams of income and fail to include the last item on the list, above, entirely: imputed income.

So, let me first go into more detail on the subject of imputed income since it is, in my opinion, perhaps the single, most beneficial aspect of owning a multi-unit residential property as opposed to a single-family house as your primary residence.

Chapter Eighteen

The Financial Alchemy of Imputed Income

In any financial issue, there are bound to be factions arguing for their perspective and opinions— human nature, right? Issues run the gamut in this regard from retirement to emergency funds and investments.

One issue, in particular, is of interest to me and it is what I call the "rent versus buy" debate. On one side, they make the point that it is a better financial decision to rent your primary residence and, on the other, they argue for exactly the opposite position: that it is better to own your primary residence.

I occasionally surf the various real estate and investment forums to discern the status of the rent versus buy debate. Passions run high on either side of the argument and the posts on these boards often devolve into name calling.

That trend is, I think, just the nature of the beast as almost every board is victimized to one extent or the other by trolls whose mission in life is to disrupt civil discourse.

But what is missing in many of the discussions on this issue is the effect that imputed income has on the analysis of the numbers bandied about. The value of imputed income is, in fact, often ignored! Any argument that does ignore imputed income is fatally flawed from the onset.

So, what is exactly is imputed income. Well, first of all, the word "imputed" means to assign a value to goods or services when the real value is unknown. Imputed income is income that is received in some form to which a value cannot be readily assigned. We do not have to assign a value to cash because the value of cash is easy to determine.

But in the rent-versus-buy debate, the imputed value we are trying to establish is that of the value of being able to live in a house rent-free. "Wait a minute!" you are thinking. "How does this guy figure you live in a house rent-free when you are making mortgage payments?"

Well, the first fact that the pro-rent crowd ignores and the single fact that you must understand in this issue is this:

Buying a piece of real property by means of a mortgage is not the same as renting one's housing.

When you rent you are paying the market value for that housing. When you have a mortgage, however, your monthly payment is the cost of acquiring the asset that property represents.

So, when you live in that property, you are paying nothing in "rent" and you are, in fact, living rent-free!

The value of the rent that you don't pay when you are buying your house is an example of what is known as, *imputed income*; that is, value you are receiving in some form other than cash.

Chapter Nineteen

The Answer Is: It Depends!

First, let me say that there is no single answer to the rent versus buy debate that is correct in every instance for every individual consumer.

The answer to whether you, personally, should buy or rent is contingent on a whole host of factors, and some of those factors will be unique to your situation.

So, anyone claiming the Holy Grail in this regard is off on the wrong foot. The correct answer is: It depends. And it depends on factors some of which are not financial. Some of the factors weighing in on the debate are purely emotional.

The simple fact of the matter is that some of us should rent for life while some of us, on the other hand, will consider renting to be throwing your money away.

Our personal residence can be both an emotional asset and a financial asset, it can be one or the other at the same time, or it can be neither, as well. Personally, I was never able feel "at home" in a rented house.

But I also realize that owning a home comes with its own challenges and costs; but that is a premium I am willing to pay for satisfying those emotions that make me want to own. Some people don't experience those same emotions; I get that.

And even before I get to the subject of imputed income, I want to mention that every financially successful individual I know either owns or has a mortgage on their personal residence. Not one person I know with a net worth in excess of one-million dollars rents their house.

Think about that and think about why that might be the case... Certainly the real estate market is battered as I write this in 2010 but I have lived through three downtowns in the market and each time prices have rebounded. This instance might be different than the others, some argue that it is, but I doubt it.

In fact, investors are flooding back into the market right now because, at a certain price point, rental property becomes a sound long-term investment; such has always been the case and the numbers don't lie.

The usual arguments against buying have to do with the costs of owning versus the costs of renting and assume all else being equal

So, let's look at a typical set of numbers based on the assumption that it would cost you twice as much to "buy" a home as it would to rent the same house in the same area—$1,000 to rent versus $2,000 to buy.

Here is where the math of those on the rent-side of the argument starts to break down because, even at twice the amount, you will come out ahead by being an owner. Why? Two reasons: Tax deductions and imputed income.

In this case, the value of the imputed income is $1,000—what the renter is paying to rent the same house. So, already you are breaking even on the purchase.

Now add to this the value of the many individual tax deductions, equity accumulation by paying down the principal balance of the mortgage, and appreciation of the value of the underlying asset, and the facts clearly favor buying; sometimes significantly so!

A buyer needs to do his or her homework and discern the costs for themselves but omitting imputed income will make the calculation, itself, incorrect and the answer, then, also incorrect.

It is hard to make a good decision based on bad data. So, if you want to make a sound decision when trying to decide for yourself whether you should buy or rent, you must include the value of imputed income in the calculation.

In the rent-versus-buy debate, both sides tend to omit pertinent facts either because their math skills are weak or they are being purposely disingenuous to bolster their case. Actually, however, doing so only weakens their case by undermining their credibility.

But the prudent buyer needs to be aware of red herrings injected into the rent versus buy debate to throw the reader off track.

Chapter Twenty

The Problem with Imputed Income

The problem with imputed income is you can't spend it. That is, you don't realize the *cash value* of living in your mortgaged house as actual cash. When you have a mortgage, you are not, technically–speaking, paying rent. In most cases, however, the money that would go to pay rent goes to pay your mortgage instead.

So, no "extra" money you can actually spend, right? But, if, on the other hand, you own a multi-unit residential property and live in one of the units as your primary residence, then it is entirely possible to realize the value of imputed income as cash!

How so? Well, if the rent you receive is equal to or more than your mortgage payment, your mortgage is, in effect, being paid for you and you get to keep that money in your pocket to spend on something else! Cool, huh?

And, if you purchase your MRP with that criteria in mind, that is, so that the rent you receive is enough to pay your mortgage, then the money you save will almost certainly offset any difference in income you might experience between working full-time and having double the free time of a four-day weekend!

I was able to do just that as I detailed in Chapter Ten, *My Real Estate Story*. And just to refresh your memory so you don't have to go flipping back through the pages, you will recall that I bought a duplex and the rent I received from the other unit paid the mortgage.

What that means is that my housing cost became zero—less than zero, actually, because I made me a profit once all streams of income were factored into the equation!

So, the line item in my budget for housing the day before I rented the other unit ($1,000) went to zero the day after I rented the apartment. And, what is most important for you to clearly realize here is this: My net income went up by the $1,000 of my income that I had previously been spending on housing.

At the time I was making about $40,000 gross and taking home (my net income) about $32,000. But my net **after** deducting my housing expense was only $20,000.

If I had switched to four-day weekends at that time, my gross would have been 75% of my previous gross or $30,000 and my net after taxes would have been $24,000 and my net after housing would have been $12,000.

> *Remember, housing is paid with after-tax income, so it comes out of your net income.*

So, by eliminating my annual housing expense, I was able to add that amount back to my net income making my revised net income $24,000.

And what that means is that, even after making the switch to the four-day weekend, my net income rose by 20%—a whopping $4,000. I could have doubled my free time **and** had more money in the bargain!

Chapter Twenty-One

Income Stream #1: Rental Income

The most obvious stream of income generated by a rental property is rent. And it is this stream of income that will provide the bulk of the cash income generated by a rental property although imputed income will also contribute a large part of the total benefits of owning rental property.

Later I will get into specific numbers of just how owning a rental can allow you to live rent-free and also reduce your income taxes to provide you even more income by avoiding the expense of paying taxes including employment taxes someday.

But there is more to rental income than you might consider at first. Rental properties are one of the few investments you can make that allow you to build "sweat equity."

Sweat equity is value that you add to the property to make it worth more. That increase in value goes right to your bottom line to grow your net worth. Sweat equity is achieved by the sweat of your brow, that is, by your labor and time.

That sweat-of-your-brow aspect is why the increase in value that results when you improve your property doing the work yourself is known as sweat equity.

For example, simple and low-cost cosmetic changes can increase the value of your property and also make it possible for you to charge a higher rent than you could if you had not made the changes.

A few examples of cosmetic changes that increase the value of a property are interior and exterior paint, landscaping, and some simple renovations such as installing a bathroom vanity.

When you, yourself, do the work associated with completing a sweat-equity project, you save the cost of labor you would otherwise have to pay. By doing that, you will also realize a higher rate of return on the money you invest in a project.

Growing the value of your investment property through the application of sweat equity is one reason why rental real estate is such a great home-based small business in support of the four-day-weekend lifestyle. The two really do go hand in hand!

When you have a four-day weekend every week, you will have plenty of time to tackle improvements and repairs around your property that will enhance the value of your investment. Time is a valuable resource, your time invested in your property, in particular.

Other investments do not allow you to leverage your time and labor to increase your equity. There is no sweat equity to be had in the stock market or when you buy gold.

And, by steadily improving your property to make it a more desirable rental, that, in turn, can allow you to demand a higher rent when compared to the competition. Sweat equity is a way to boost rents above what they will rise based solely on inflation.

Improvements made to your property that will allow you to charge as little as an extra $50 a month in a fourplex building will add an extra $1,800 to your annual income!

In my rental agreements, I add a clause informing the renter that the rent will increase every year. By doing that, the tenant knows the increase is coming and, so, will not be surprised or disgruntled. Disgruntled tenants are tenants who might just decide to move out!

Writing an annual increase into my leases is also a way to make sure that my income increases every year to keep up with inflation.

Over time, an annual increase in my gross income of only a few percentage points is enough to grow my income considerably. And, knowing I have the increase coming, I am also able to plan my finances better.

Chapter Twenty-Two

Income Stream #2: Depreciation

The money you will save on taxes by owning rental real estate could well be enough to eliminate some or maybe even all of the income differential between the rat race and the four-day weekend. Rental real estate provides what is, perhaps, the last great, no-cost income tax deduction. That deduction is known as "depreciation."

The IRS assumes, in your favor, that as a building ages it loses value until, at some point, it will be worth zero. The IRS also assumes that the time-frame for this depreciation to occur is 27.5 years. So, to compensate the income property owner for this loss of value, that owner is allowed to deduct the amount of that annual depreciation from their taxes every year.

Sounds a little complicated, I know, so let me put it into numbers for you:

First, we need to make some assumptions to detail the numbers involved; in this case, let's assume that we purchase a fourplex (four individual units) for $200,000.

The IRS does not allow you to depreciate the value of the land on which a property sits because, according to them, land does not depreciate. We could argue that but, really, it is easier just to accept their premise in this regard.

So, now, we need to assign a value to land on which our fourplex is constructed. The higher the value you do assign to the land, the less the value of the building and, so, the less you will be able to deduct as depreciation every year. And you should also know that someday the IRS might ask you to explain how you arrived at the value you do assign to the land.

In most cases, however, there is an easy rule of thumb: The IRS will not usually question any valuation in the range of ten to twenty percent. I, personally, use the twenty percent figure and the lower the value you assign the more likely it is that your valuation will be the subject of an IRS audit!

Now we need to remember that you are living in one unit and, so, the tax law does not allow you to depreciate that portion of the building. Since this is a fourplex, and you are living in one of the four units, twenty-five percent of the deduction is not applicable.

OK. $200,000 times 80% equals a value of $160,000 assigned to the building; $160,000 times (.75) equals $120,000 and that is the amount subject to depreciation over 27.5 years.

$120,000 divided by 27.5 equals an annual tax-deduction of $4,363. If we assume the same 20% tax-rate from previous examples, $4,363 of depreciation deduction will save you just about $875 a year and will be realized as cash.

But this is not the end of the tax-breaks we get as income property owners!

You can also deduct (assuming the same numbers as in the last example) that same 75% of all expenses you incur in maintaining the property. This deduction is far-ranging and extremely inclusive. Again, you don't want to go crazy here but, if you have ever been a homeowner in the past, you know how these expenses add up!

And there are expenses that you can include that you might not consider at first such as car mileage to go to and from the local hardware store to buy property maintenance supplies and, even, the cost of the hotel in a different town if you conduct any business while you are there that has to do with your income property business.

But these expenses all cost you actual money from your pocket. And although you will likely recapture these costs in the form of rent, they are not the "free" deduction provided by the depreciation "expense."

I think I'll print up a bumper sticker to read:

Got Depreciation?

Chapter Twenty-Three

Income Stream #3: Tax Savings from Mortgage Interest Deductions

Another tax benefit you receive when you own rental property is that you can deduct interest paid on the mortgage of your property.

Generally speaking, any MRP with more than two units is likely to cost more than you would spend on a single-family residence. When you purchase an MRP, however, the projected rents can be used to qualify for the mortgage.

The larger the mortgage on your MRP, the more interest you will have to deduct as an expense. And, perhaps, the greatest benefit of a tax *deduction* is that it can reduce not only the taxes you pay on earned income but on passive income, as well!

This, in turn, *can* give you more spending power and will go a long way towards the goal of making the difference in buying power before and after you make the switch to the four-day weekend as small as possible, if not eliminate it entirely!

Keeping track of your interest deduction will require very little bookkeeping on your part. The financial institution holding your mortgage is required by law to send you a tax form every year that will tell you exactly how much interest you paid in the previous year.

Figuring out your depreciation deduction, on the other hand, will be up to you but once you figure out how much depreciation you can deduct every year, that figure will stay the same for the next twenty-seven (+) years or until you sell your property.

The thing is, you will only be able to claim a portion of both the depreciation and mortgage interest tax deduction when you live in one of the units of the property. The portion you are able to claim is equal to the percentage of the property that is used as a rental.

What that means is, for example, if you have a duplex and you live in one of the two units, only one-half of the property is a rental. In that case, you could only deduct 50% of the mortgage interest and 50% of the depreciation expense.

But what that also means is that the more units the property has, the larger percentage of the respective deduction you can claim as a business expense.

So, if the property is a fourplex, you will be able to claim 75% of each deduction as a business expense. This is one argument for owning a three or four unit property.

Of course, whatever portion of the mortgage interest deduction you cannot claim as a rental expense, you can still claim as a personal write-off if you itemize your personal deductions.

Chapter Twenty-Four

*Income Stream # 4: Equity Growth through
Principal Reduction*

The third stream of income listed is principal reduction. "Principal" is the original loan amount on the underlying mortgage used to acquire the asset. Every time you make a mortgage payment, a part of that payment is applied "against" the balance of the principal and, so, you owe less and own more of the underlying asset.

Eventually, exactly when determined by the term of your mortgage loan, the loan will be paid in-full and you will own the property outright.

This is an important consideration because, once the property is all yours, so is all the income it produces!

A mortgage can work for you or against you and which type of mortgage is best for you is dependent on your particular financial situation when you acquire the mortgage and your long-term goals, as well. There might be other considerations as well but those are usually the two most important.

The best way to think of a mortgage is in five-year blocks. In each block, a percentage of your mortgage payment goes to pay down the principal and the rest goes to pay interest. Now this is where it gets interesting:

In the first five-year block of a thirty-year mortgage with an interest rate of six percent, less than seven percent of the total of all the payments made in those first five years will go to reduce principal, the rest is "lost" to interest.

Let's look at a mortgage of $100,000 with an interest rate of six percent, for example:

The monthly payment, principal and interest, will be $599.55. The total of payments for one year will be $7,194.60.

The total of payments during the first five-year block will be $35,973.

However, at the end of five years, the principal balance is still over $93,000; $93,054.36, to be exact. And what that means is that you paid over $29,000 in interest!

Look—it will always hurt a little to pay interest even when the pain is mollified a little by the leverage you gain by paying it. But paying eighty cents on the dollar is still extreme, mollified or not!

A thirty-year mortgage, because it is so expensive in terms of interest paid during the first and second five-year block, is a sort of "mortgage-of-last-resort" in my book.

To make my point, let's look at the principal and interest numbers for the first five-year block of a twenty-year mortgage.

Chapter Twenty-Five

Interest is Interesting!

Assuming the same facts—a $100,000 mortgage at 6% interest—your payments on a twenty-year mortgage will be $716.43—about 16% more than the $599.55 payment on a thirty-year mortgage but less than $120 a month in real dollars, percentages aside.

Total of payments after one year will be $8,561.16 and after five years, $42,850.80.

But your principal balance at the end of that time will be $84,899.60. In other words (or, rather, in other numbers!), your principal has been reduced by $15,100.40: A full 35% of the total of your monthly mortgage payments has been applied to principal compared to just 19% during the same amount of time in a thirty-year mortgage—almost twice as much!

Now, mortgage interest is deductible but the benefits of that deduction are over-rated as far as I am concerned.

Still, it is most often the case that people finance a home purchase with a thirty-year mortgage in order to qualify for the loan and to make the monthly payment more affordable—that is—to make it lower.

In the end, the mortgage you select will be decided by balancing your financial realities and goals, as I mentioned previously. I recommend the book, *How to Unscramble Your Nest Egg*, written by John J. Cunningham for more information on selecting the mortgage that is right for you. That is the book that opened my eyes on this subject.

Also covered in that book are strategies to "buy back" the time you bought when you first acquired your mortgage; another concept well-worth reading more about.

Chapter Twenty-Six

Income Stream #5: Appreciation

If you're not familiar with real estate investing, the words used in the title of this chapter are probably not familiar to you but both principal reduction and appreciation are basic concepts in field.

Appreciation is the term given to the increase in value (above the purchase price) of an underlying asset; in this case real estate.

The value of real estate had, historically, gone up and down on a steadily climbing trend-line, like the relative position of a yo-yo being swung by a boy walking up a moderately inclined hill.

As I write these words in mid-2010, real estate is well into a historic correction after an equally historic run-up in prices ended in the bursting of the asset-class bubble of earth-shattering proportions.

Neither the run-up nor crash was based on fundamentals of the underlying asset. Instead, both were the result of some banking failures, the likes of which we are unlikely to see again for decades, if ever.

But also as I write this, the market is recovering and real estate investors, as always, are the first to jump back in because numbers don't lie: Real estate will always be a sound investment at a certain price point; specifically, when acquisition costs and the benefits of ownership including rental income provide a reasonable return.

Historically, real estate enjoys periods of moderate appreciation of around five percent between the occasional down-cycle and it looks like we are now heading back to that historical averages although it still might take a couple of years to get there.

But real estate is a unique investment for the average investor because it is the only asset-class where it is possible for the average investor to reap the benefits of financial leverage without incurring an inordinate amount of risk to do so.

That leverage is the result of gaining beneficial use of an asset worth several times the cost of gaining that beneficial use. For example, when you buy a property for $200,000 with a twenty percent down payment, you have benefited from the use of financial leverage.

Where that leverage exerts itself to the investor's benefit is when the underlying asset, the real estate in this case, appreciates.

For example, if that same property appreciates, that is, if it goes up in market value by five percent in one year (which is about the average rate of appreciation in residential real estate) that appreciation ($10,000) represents a return on your investment ($40,000) of twenty-five percent.

The amount of leverage available to an investor in the typical real estate investment is one reason why real estate has made more millionaires than any other type of investment.

Chapter Twenty-Seven

Another Random Walk Down Main Street

Obtaining a mortgage to buy a multi-unit residential property is likely to be the single toughest aspect of making the switch to four-day weekends but "tough" only in the sense that getting a mortgage is something of a pain in the neck.

But, remember, this only applies if you decide to implement this part of the plan!

It is entirely possible that you will be able to make up the difference in income by other means such as simply reducing your expenses. But, if you do decide to pursue this aspect of the plan, you really do need to do your homework!

And it could definitely work to your benefit if you decide whether or not to implement this strategy before making the switch to the four-day weekend. Why?

Simply because it is likely that you will be in a better position to qualify for a mortgage while you still have a full-time income.

And, if you presently own a single-family house (or "own" the mortgage on it), you might want to consider selling it if the profits from doing so would fund your purchase of a multi-unit residential property. (Or fund the down payment, anyway!)

Selling a house could be tough in this market, however, and is almost never a quick and easy proposition, in any market regardless. So, implementing this part of the plan is not a consideration to be taken lightly.

But you can, absolutely, make the switch without implementing this strategy, as well. It is just that the benefits of being a landlord *can* be so financially rewarding that, for me, it is difficult to pass up the opportunity.

If you, likewise, find the prospect interesting, I suggest you take a few steps to educate yourself on the subject of purchasing and owning multi-unit residential housing. The first thing I recommend you do is read a few good books on the subject.

There are hundreds, maybe thousands, of books on the subject available online at sites like amazon.com. But to get you started, here are the titles of the five books that I recommend every beginning real estate investor should read:

How I Turned $1,000 into a Million in Real Estate—in My Spare Time!

Written by William Nickerson, this book was originally published in 1959! It is an absolute classic but can be hard to find.

Rental Houses for the Successful Small Investor

Written by Suzanne P. Thomas, this book is one of my personal favorites in that it has no-hype or fluff. The author de-mystifies the real estate investing process and makes it very easy to understand. I would recommend this as the first book to read on the subject simply because she makes the information so accessible.

The Income Stream

Written by Robert M. Goodman, this book is a must-read! The author goes into depth on the math of how to calculate the return on a real estate investment. The book also includes an in-depth analysis of four of the five income streams that real estate can provide the investor.

Financial Independence

Written by David J. Grzesiek, this book covers properties in the lower income spectrum. The author used to present seminars on the material in this book before the real estate seminar-business turned into the racket it is today; he was a pioneer in other words.

Landlording

Written by Leigh Robinson and the absolute classic in its field! The number one resource on the subject of profitably managing rental income property and it will give you a taste for the nuts and bolts of doing so, as well.

Chapter Twenty-Eight

The Freedom of Shared Spaces

So, what does the theory of owning a MRP look like when applied in the real world? I already gave you one example, my own, but there are countless others being realized everyday across the country.

Let's say you buy a fourplex for $200,000 in Phoenix, AZ, where buying a property like that is entirely possible and not a stretch at all as I write this (2010). I know it is possible because I visit the website, Realtor.com, all the time to keep up with the marketplace for just this sort of properties.

I find this property at the website and I call the listing agent who tells me that each unit is six-hundred square feet with two-bedrooms and one bathroom. Each unit, she continues, rents for $550.

This kind of market research is not rocket science and you can do it, right now, yourself. Simply go to the website and search in your area to find what is available. Then you call the listing agent, that is, the agent that is representing the seller, and ask one simple questions:

What is the rental income of each individual unit?

With that single piece of information you can get a very good idea of whether or not the property will allow you to achieve the goal of reducing your cost of housing to zero.

To determine whether or not any property will do that, you simply compare the gross monthly rental income minus the amount of the monthly mortgage payment and expenses and, if the result zero or greater, there is a strong possibility that it will.

For example, using the numbers already mentioned, we have a $200,000 fourplex. The monthly rental income from the three units we are renting (remember, we are living in one unit) would be equal to $550 x 3 or $1,650 a month. Now, we need to deduct expenses from that figure to determine net income:

The industry standard for estimating expenses not related to principal and interest on the mortgage is 30% of gross *rental* income:

$1,650 times 30% equals $495, meaning that this property will net $1,155 after expenses ($1,650 total of rents minus $495 expenses): That $1,155 is the amount you will have "left" to pay the mortgage and any amount above the monthly mortgage payment is your profit.

In this case, if we assume a 20% down payment ($40,000) and a thirty-year mortgage term at 5% interest, the result will be a monthly mortgage payment of $858.91.

Based on this very simple calculation, the property in this example would not only allow you to live rent-free, it would actually provide a positive cash-flow of almost $300 a month! (Net Income minus Mortgage Payment)

That monthly cash flow ($300) plus the imputed income of the free rent you are receiving ($550) provides an annual return of almost 26% on your down payment! Almost unbelievable, I know, but here is the calculation:

[$550 (imputed income) + $300 (monthly positive rental income) = ($850) x 12 (months) = $10,200/$40,000 (down payment) = .255 (25.5%)]

And, as if that return is not reason enough to own a MRP, owning a rental property is, in fact, a small business that you can grow and cultivate as the years go by—a business that you can choose to expand by acquiring more properties.

Now, if you manage the debt on that property correctly, you can plan to have the mortgage paid-off by the time you are eligible for Social Security and by doing so, the income from your rentals, now free and clear of any mortgage, will provide you the means to enjoy a more financially secure retirement.

Are the actual steps to get there a bit more complicated than they are presented in my quick review of the numbers? Absolutely! But are they so complicated that the complexity of it should stop you from achieving the goal of rent-free living and a secure retirement? Absolutely not!

People enter the rental business every day. And I mean people just like you and me! I did it when I didn't even realize I was doing it. Are there pitfalls to avoid? Absolutely! But they are well-known and the information is available that will help you avoid them.

The best place to start learning about your local real estate market is at the website, *www.realtor.com*. There you will be able to see what properties are available in your area and at what cost.

If you type the name of the city in the "Location" search box, the default search parameters are for single-family houses and condominiums. To search for multi-family homes, go to the advanced search feature and select that option.

Each individual property on that site is known as a "listing." The seller of each property you see there will be represented by a real estate agent, known as the "listing agent."

Once you have gone to that website and seen the properties there, the next step will be to actually visit a few of those properties yourself.

At first, you might want to just drive-by the listings to see what they look like from the outside and to determine which properties appeal to you enough to warrant a look at what's inside.

To get inside those properties, you will need a real estate agent—either the listing agent or, better yet, a "buyer's" agent. You see, the *listing* agent is required, by law, to represent the best interests of the seller. A buyer's agent has no such obligation and a more "neutral" agent will most often be in your own best interests.

A buyer's agent can be any real estate agent other than the listing agent. I am also of the opinion that, ideally, your buyer's agent should not even be affiliated with the same company as the listing agent.

It is likely that you will be spending a considerable amount of time with your agent to find a property to purchase. But all real estate agents, just like all people in general, will have their own unique personality and work-style and not every agent will be someone with whom you will, necessarily, want to work.

That being a consideration in selecting a buyer's agent, I would recommend you not commit to the first buyer's agent you meet. Instead, take the time to meet with and interview a few, at least, in an attempt to find one with whom you feel comfortable.

Part Three

How to Save Money Tax-Free

Chapter Twenty-Nine

How to Unscramble Your Nest Egg

A concern that many of us share is that of saving for retirement. Most often, the reason for our concern is the fact that we know that we are not saving enough to make a financially comfortable retirement possible.

The fact is, as a nation, we save on average zero or, even, less than zero depending on whose statistics you care to believe.

Oddly enough, in 2008, about the time the country slipped into recession, the national personal savings rate actually increased. No big deal, really, since the rate, itself, remained insufficient to achieve financial independence by retirement age. So, based on our failure as a nation to build sufficient retirement savings, we are right to be worried.

This was a big concern for me, as well. How, I wondered, could saving for retirement and the four-day weekend possibly co-exist? I mean, if people aren't saving enough to retire when they work five days-a-week, wouldn't working less mean saving less?

A financially secure retirement does not happen by accident—it takes planning. And if I could find a plan to work less and live more, I was confident that I could also find a plan to really retire (no work at all!) at some point in the future, if I wanted to or it became necessary, for whatever reason.

Obviously, however, budgeting to save for retirement would be an additional cost that could well torpedo a plan to switch to the four-day weekend. I still managed to find the money, however.

A part of the traditional retirement plan is to have one's house paid for by the time you plan to retire. By doing so, you remove that line item from your budget and make retirement cost that much less.

In the last section of this book, I explained how to reduce your housing cost to zero or, even, how to turn a profit by making your primary residence a multi-unit residential property. And, as we will explore, that same strategy will also go a long way towards funding a comfortable retirement.

Chapter Thirty

Planning for Financial Independence

If you will recall, I have already conceded that part-time jobs usually pay less per hour than full-time jobs for work that is essentially the same. Well, it is also often the case that the benefits offered part-time employees will not be the same as those offered a full-time employee by the same employer.

And, perhaps, the area where the issue of benefits should concern you the most, as you consider making the switch to the four-day weekend, is when it comes to benefits having to do with retirement plans.

Most of us will achieve the financial independence required to retire using what is known as the three-legs of the retirement *stool*: Social Security, income from savings and investments, and benefits from a retirement plan.

And the retirement plan that is most likely to provide that third leg of the stool for most Americans in the future will be the 401(k) Individual Retirement Account (IRA).

The name for the retirement plan, itself, "401(k)," comes from the section of the Internal Revenue Code where the specifics of the plan are detailed [Section 401(k)].

401(k) plans are usually *administered* by the employer for their employees but, and this is a very BIG but here, it is the employee that must decide how to invest the funds in their IRA.

Employees can choose to participate or not in the plan but if they do the employer will usually match the employee deposits up to some defined amount. The employer deposits are known as "contributions" and it is why the 401k IRA is known as a defined-*contribution* plan.

The decision to offer employees a 401(k) plan and/or matching funds, however, is largely at the discretion of the employer and not all part-time employees will be eligible to participate in an employer's plan—that's the first part of bad news in regards to working part-time and retirement benefits but it doesn't end there.

Contributions to a 401(k) IRA are limited to a certain percentage of your income and what that means is that, if you work part-time instead of full-time, you will earn less and so the absolute amount of dollars saved will be proportionally less, as well.

But the less any particular leg of the retirement stool can be expected to contribute, the more retirement income will need to be provided by the remaining two legs of the stool, in this case, Social Security and personal savings.

The thing is, the less you earn, the less you will pay into Social Security, as well. So, ultimately, the largest slice of your retirement income pie will need to come from your savings and investments.

But you can go a long way towards securing that extra income simply by planning to be mortgage-free by the time you are eligible for Social Security.

Chapter Thirty-One

How to Feather Your Nest Egg

If the term of your mortgage extends past your planned retirement date, then it will be necessary to "pre-pay" or "pay down" your mortgage to align the two dates.

However, money you invest to pay down your mortgage is highly leveraged to your benefit. For one thing, it will reduce the total amount of interest you will pay to acquire the asset your house represents and, so, lower your acquisition cost. And each dollar you pay down your mortgage increases your equity and, so, your total net worth, as well.

And, although those extra amounts paid to pay-down your mortgage are made with after tax dollars (net income), once they are put to work that way, they will never be taxed again. In that way, that is, as an investment made with net income, investing in equity is like investing in a Roth Individual Retirement Account (IRA).

A Roth IRA is different than a "traditional" 401k IRA in that contributions made to a Roth IRA are made from net income while contributions to a 401k IRA are made from gross income and you will pay no income tax on those contributions until you withdraw them.

That is why you will save present-day tax-dollars by saving in a 401k IRA. But most smart money these days is going into Roth IRAs. Why? Because most people assume that tax-rates are going to continue to rise and they would rather pay less taxes now than more taxes later.

In both types of accounts, the money in the account grows tax-free but in a Roth IRA you will pay no taxes when you withdraw your contributions. You will, however, pay income taxes when you withdraw contributions from a traditional IRA account. And, in both types of accounts, you will also pay income tax on any interest the account earns.

Money paid as extra principal on your mortgage is exactly like money invested in a Roth IRA, only better. First, the similarities: Both investments are made from after tax net income and both accounts are allowed to grow tax-free.

But the difference between the two is this and it is major:

As of this edition, profits from the sale of your primary residence are tax-free up to $250,000 for a single person and up to $500,000 for a couple. When your primary residence is an MRP, some portion of the proceeds from its sale will be tax-free, as well. There is no such tax-free treatment of the profits realized in a Roth IRA.

What this means to you is that your multi-unit residential property might be the single best retirement plan available! And it can be the basis for your retirement planning in a couple of ways.

One, you can plan to sell your property when you retire and use the proceeds to fund your retirement along with your other retirement income.

Or, two, you can keep the property and plan to have it paid off by the time you retire so that all the income it generates will be available to you as gross income; and it will be that income, plus your Social Security check and any retirement plan income, that will be the total amount you will have to finance your retirement.

Of course, you might never want to retire. I mean, after all, you're only working three days a week! Or, at the very least, you might decide to keep working longer than you would have if you were still trapped in the rat race.

In which case, you can delay drawing your Social Security benefits which will mean they will be that much more when you finally do choose to receive them. All in all, a win-win-win situation for you!

Chapter Thirty-Two

Living the Free Life: One Last Real World Example

So, is it possible to escape the rat race to work less and live more? Is the four-day weekend financially possible? I'm glad you asked! In a couple of previous examples, I have showed you that making the switch could cost 10%, maybe 15%, or maybe zero. Now, I want to make the case one more time:

In constructing the following example, I did not assume someone working three-days a week in some highly-paid professional career. I just figured that the "family unit" (FU) consisted of two adults each making $10 an hour, not much more than minimum-wage, and each working three, ten-hour days-a-week.

The income of this FU would be 30 x $10 times the two working adults for a total of $600 a week before taxes. $600 a week times the 52 weeks in a year equals $31,200. That amount is just about one-half of the national average for all family units as reported by the Bureau of Labor Statistics ($63,091)—49.45% to be exact.

Now, without any hocus-pocus and using those same BLS statistics, and keeping in mind that you don't need to replace income you weren't spending in support of your lifestyle, we can refigure that 49.45% based on the net effect of taxes. The BLS reports an average tax-load of slightly over 21% but we will use 21% in the following computation:

First, we know the net income after taxes in the representative BLS family unit is $49,638

To figure the net income after taxes of the 4DW couple, we multiply their gross income by that 21% figure to arrive at their tax-bill and subtract that figure from their gross income:

$31,200 times .21 = $6,552

$31,200 minus $6,552 = $24,648 Net After-Tax Income

But, remember, you don't have to replace income you were earning but not spending back in your rat race days; in this case, the difference between pre and post-4DW taxes. Before, you were spending $13,453 and after that amount goes down to $6,552.

$13453 minus $6552 = $6901

That $6,091 is money you will not need to replace post-4DW because it was not going to support your income. The way I like to look at this is to "add" this amount to your post-4DW income to figure the "actual" difference between pre and post 4DW income:

$24,648 plus 6,901 = $31,549

So, what just happened? Well, your post-4DW income just went "up" to just about 64% of pre-4DW net income!

But, wait, it gets better:

If we assume that this couple follows the strategy and that, by owning a multi-unit property instead of a single-family residence (purchased and financed while they were still both working full-time jobs), they have zero housing cost (mortgage principal and interest or rent), the difference in net income between the two family-units is cut to almost zero:

$49,638 minus $16,920 = $32,718

[(national average net income) minus (national average cost of housing, either mortgage principal and interest or rent) = $32,718]

$32,718 minus $31,549 = $1,169

Savings realized by working four fewer days a week will almost certainly add another five percent to your actual post-4DW net and turn what, at first, looked like an unmanageable cut in pay to the point where you are actually earning more than you were earning before!

And, remember, this assumes a wage of not much more than the minimum wage—just $10 an hour. If you are able to earn more than that, the difference will actually be a net-gain in your take-home pay!

So, is it possible to work less, live more, and enjoy the freedom of the four-day weekend? Look over the numbers just detailed and judge for yourself. As you have just seen, and based on real world numbers, it is likely that the four-day weekend won't cost you anything at all!

So, why not double your free time? I mean, after all, it might just not cost you a dime to do so!

Chapter Thirty-Three

Random Notes from the Four-Day Front

I mentioned before that, after achieving total financial independence and leaving the rat race entirely, I had so much free time on my hand that I found myself battling boredom at times.

I even considered going back to a full-time job. Instead, I settled into the four-day weekend and the three-day workweek. But guess what? Even though I had my hobbies and other pursuits, the four-day weekend still provides a lot of free-time!

Certainly, I did not need any more paid employment but I felt as if I could "afford" the time to give back to my community. That is when I came up with an idea: Give away one-half of one day! I decided to find a local organization with a mission I could support as a volunteer for four hours a week or so.

It was no problem finding that organization and the "work" I perform as a volunteer is rewarding in a way that paid-employment and even time spent on my own pursuits is not.

If you will remember, earlier in the book I advised you to have a plan for how you will spend your time once you make the switch to the four day weekend; planning to volunteer some of your time is an ideal use of the most precious resource we each possess—our time! So, think about it and plan to give away one-half day!

Now, I want to change the subject to a more macro-perspective of the subject of the four-day weekend. Right now the US is experiencing one of the highest unemployment rates in recent memory. Jobs are at a premium.

When you decide to trade away ten hours of paid employment for the sheer luxury of the four-day weekend, those ten hours will not go un-worked, someone else will get paid to do that work. What that means on a larger scale is that every time four of us make the switch we will have "created" the equivalent of one more full-time job.

Afterword

Afterword

It is my hope that, eventually, more (and more!) American workers will choose to take the rewards of increased productivity in the form of increased leisure time.

That is, I hope that we will choose more free time to do with what we will, instead of working more paid hours simply to buy more *stuff* and if for no other reason other than the data are pointing to the fact that we simply can't continue to consume at the same level without the system breaking at some point.

Making the switch to the four-day weekend can be as simple as simply cutting back a little and if you do that, cut back a little, I mean, just maybe the result will be that you will walk a bit more lightly on the planet.

And, now, in the hope that we all might walk a bit more lightly someday, I leave you with the words of the prophet of Walden Pond, Henry David Thoreau:

Simplify, simplify, simplify.

And with the words of Buddha:

If you would seek peace,
stop chasing so many things.

Thank you for reading this book.

About the Author

Wallace R. Curiel is the author of several books, owner of Transcendental Media Group, and publisher of TMG Books and the website of the same name.

He is the owner of the trademark property:

Is It Wednesday Yet?™